Mochi-Celeste
GOES TO HAWAII

Written and illustrated by Edgar & Yuriko Justus

On Board ➡

ARE WE THERE YET?

DAY 1
in Paradise

NOT GOOD ENOUGH

DAY 2

in Paradise

ALREADY

MASTERED

DAY 3
in Paradise

DAY 4
in Paradise

DAY 5

in Paradise

DAY 6
in Paradise

DAY 7
in Paradise

DAY 8

in Paradise

DAY 9

in Paradise

DAY 10

in Paradise

NEVER SATISFIED

DAY 11
in Paradise

Now I'm
HUNGRY

DAY 12

in Paradise

Found a
SHADY SPOT

On Board

I DESERVE
FIRST CLASS

Home Sweet Home

I NEED A

VACATION

Talk Story Bookstore, LLC
PO Box 528, Hanapepe, Hawaii 96716

www.mochiceleste.com

21 22 23 24 25 WHO 6 5 4 3 2 1
First Edition, 2019
Second Revised Edition, 2021

    Library of Meowness Catalog-in-Publication Data
Justus, Edgar; Kihara, Yuriko; Justus, Yuriko,
    [Mochi-Celeste. Hawaii. Humor.]
    Mochi-Celeste : Hawaii, 2019, 2021/ Edgar Justus and Yuriko Kihara (Yuriko Justus)
    Collection of humorous sayings collected with drawings of Mochi-Celeste in Hawaii, based on
Celeste_the_Cat_Boss of Instagram fame, located at Talk Story Bookstore in Hanapepe, Kauai, Hawaii.
ISBN: 978-1-0878-5356-7
1. Mochi-Celeste. 2. Humor. 3. Justus, Edgar. 4. Kihara, Yuriko. 4a. Justus, Yuriko. 5. Cats.
6. Hawaii. 7. Hawaiian Islands. 8. Vacations. 9. Misery. 10. Meow. I. Title.

PN7734.C01W8088675309
170.1'016-dc50
1087853567

Design: Edgar Justus and Yuriko Kihara (Yuriko Justus)